FREE DVD

From Stress to Success DVD
from Trivium Test Prep

Dear Customer,

Thank you for purchasing from Trivium Test Prep! Whether you're looking to join the military, get into college, or advance your career, we're honored to be a part of your journey.

To show our appreciation (and to help you relieve a little of that test-prep stress), we're offering a **FREE CEN Essential Test Tips DVD*** by Trivium Test Prep. Our DVD includes 35 test preparation strategies that will help keep you calm and collected before and during your big exam. All we ask is that you email us your feedback and describe your experience with our product. Amazing, awful, or just so-so: we want to hear what you have to say!

To receive your **FREE CEN Test Tips DVD**, please email us at 5star@triviumtestprep.com. Include "Free 5 Star" in the subject line and the following information in your email:

1. The title of the product you purchased.
2. Your rating from 1 – 5 (with 5 being the best).
3. Your feedback about the product, including how our materials helped you meet your goals and ways in which we can improve our products.
4. Your full name and shipping address so we can send your **FREE CEN Essential Test Tips DVD**.

If you have any questions or concerns please feel free to contact us directly at 5star@triviumtestprep.com. Thank you, and good luck with your studies!

* Please note that the free DVD is not included with this book. To receive the free DVD, please follow the instructions above.

CEN TERMS AND DEFINITIONS

E. M. Falgout

TABLE OF CONTENTS

INTRODUCTION

Congratulations on choosing to take the Certified Emergency Nurse (CEN) Exam! Passing the CEN is an important step forward in your nursing career.

The BCEN Certification Process

The **Certified Emergency Nurse (CEN) Exam** is developed by the **Board of Certification for Emergency Nursing (BCEN)** as part of its certification program for emergency nurses. The CEN measures the nursing skills necessary to excel as a nurse in an emergency department. To qualify for the exam, you must have a current Registered Nurse license in the United States or its territories. The BCEN also recommends that you have at least two years of nursing experience in an emergency department. There's no level of experience that's *required* for the exam, but many nurses find that the practical knowledge they have acquired while working in the ED is vital to passing the exam.

Once you have met the qualifications and passed the exam, you will have your CEN certification, and you may use the credentials as long as your certification is valid. You will need to recertify every four years. You can earn your recertification by taking continuing education courses or by retaking the exam. If you are taking the exam for recertification, you must submit your application 91 days before your certification lapses. You must then pass the exam within the 90-day testing window.

CEN Questions and Timing

The CEN consists of **175 questions**. Only 150 of these questions are scored; 25 are unscored, or *pretest* questions. These questions are included by the BCEN to test their suitability for inclusion in future tests. You'll have no way of knowing which questions are unscored, so treat every question like it counts.

The questions on the CEN are multiple-choice with four answer choices. Some questions will include exhibits such as ECG reading strips or laboratory results. The CEN has **no guess penalty**. That is, if you answer a question incorrectly, no points are deducted from your score; you simply do not get credit for that question. Therefore, you should always guess if you do not know the answer to a question.

You will have **3 hours** to complete the test. During this time you will also need to complete the BCEN Examination Rules and Regulations Agreement. You may take breaks at any point during the exam, but you will not be given extra time, and you cannot access personal items (other than medications).

CEN Content Areas

The BCEN develops its exams based on feedback from emergency nursing professionals about the nursing concepts and skills that are most important to their work. This feedback has been used to develop an exam framework that emphasizes the assessment, diagnosis, and treatment of conditions emergency nurses are likely to encounter in the ED.

The framework is broken down into seven sections loosely based on human body systems and one section devoted to professional issues. The table below gives the breakdown of the questions on the exam, and the content outline objectives are listed below the table.

Quick Summary of CEN Test Sections	
Section	**Approx. No. of Questions**

1.	Cardiovascular Emergencies	23
2.	Respiratory Emergencies	19
3.	Neurological Emergencies	19
4.	Gastrointestinal, Genitourinary, Gynecology, and Obstetrical Emergencies	24
5.	Psychosocial and Medical Emergencies	29
6.	Maxillofacial, Ocular, Orthopedic, and Wound Emergencies	24
7.	Environment and Toxicology Emergencies, and Communicable Diseases	18
8.	Professional Issues	19
Total		**175 questions**

CEN Content Outline

CARDIOVASCULAR EMERGENCIES

- Acute coronary syndrome
- Aneurysm/dissection
- Cardiopulmonary arrest
- Dysrhythmias
- Endocarditis
- Heart failure
- Hypertension
- Pericardial tamponade
- Pericarditis
- Peripheral vascular disease
- Thromboembolic disease
- Trauma
- Shock (cardiogenic and obstructive)

RESPIRATORY EMERGENCIES

- Aspiration
- Asthma
- Chronic obstructive pulmonary disease (COPD)
- Infections
- Inhalation injuries
- Obstruction
- Pleural effusion
- Pneumothorax
- Pulmonary edema, noncardiac
- Pulmonary embolus
- Respiratory distress syndrome
- Trauma

NEUROLOGICAL EMERGENCIES

- Alzheimer's disease/dementia
- Chronic neurological disorders
- Guillain-Barré syndrome
- Headache
- Increased intracranial pressure (ICP)
- Meningitis
- Seizure disorders
- Shunt dysfunctions
- Spinal cord injuries, including neurogenic shock
- Stroke (ischemic or hemorrhagic)
- Transient ischemic attack (TIA)
- Trauma

GASTROINTESTINAL EMERGENCIES

- Acute abdomen
- Bleeding
- Cholecystitis
- Cirrhosis
- Diverticulitis
- Esophageal varices
- Esophagitis
- Foreign bodies
- Gastritis
- Gastroenteritis
- Hepatitis
- Hernia
- Inflammatory bowel disease
- Intussusception
- Obstructions
- Pancreatitis
- Trauma
- Ulcers

GENITOURINARY EMERGENCIES

- Foreign bodies
- Infection
- Priapism
- Renal calculi
- Testicular torsion
- Trauma
- Urinary retention

GYNECOLOGY EMERGENCIES

- Bleeding/dysfunction (vaginal)
- Foreign bodies
- Hemorrhage
- Infection
- Ovarian cyst
- Sexual assault/battery
- Trauma

OBSTETRICAL EMERGENCIES

- Abruptio placenta
- Ectopic pregnancy
- Emergent delivery
- Hemorrhage
- Hyperemesis gravidarum
- Neonatal resuscitation
- Placenta previa
- Postpartum infection
- Preeclampsia, eclampsia, HELLP syndrome
- Preterm labor
- Threatened/spontaneous abortion
- Trauma

PSYCHOSOCIAL EMERGENCIES

- Abuse and neglect
- Aggressive/violent behavior
- Anxiety/panic
- Bipolar disorder
- Depression

- Homicidal ideation
- Psychosis
- Situational crisis
- Suicidal ideation

MEDICAL EMERGENCIES

- Allergic reactions and anaphylaxis
- Blood dyscrasias
- Disseminated intravascular coagulation (DIC)
- Electrolyte/fluid imbalance
- Endocrine conditions
- Fever
- Immunocompromise
- Renal failure
- Sepsis and septic shock

MAXILLOFACIAL EMERGENCIES

- Abscess
- Acute vestibular dysfunction
- Dental conditions
- Epistaxis
- Facial nerve disorders
- Foreign bodies
- Infections
- Ruptured tympanic membrane
- Temporomandibular joint (TMJ) dislocation
- Trauma

OCULAR EMERGENCIES

- Abrasions
- Burns
- Foreign bodies
- Glaucoma
- Infections
- Retinal artery occlusion
- Retinal detachment
- Trauma
- Ulcerations/keratitis

ORTHOPEDIC EMERGENCIES

- Amputation
- Compartment syndrome
- Contusions
- Costochondritis
- Foreign bodies
- Fractures/dislocations
- Inflammatory conditions
- Joint effusion
- Low back pain
- Osteomyelitis
- Strains/sprains
- Trauma

WOUND EMERGENCIES

- Abrasions
- Avulsions
- Foreign bodies

- Infections
- Injection injuries
- Lacerations
- Missile injuries
- Pressure ulcers
- Puncture wounds
- Trauma

ENVIRONMENT EMERGENCIES

- Burns
- Chemical exposure
- Electrical injuries
- Envenomation emergencies
- Food poisoning
- Parasite and fungal infestations
- Radiation exposure
- Submersion injury
- Temperature-related emergencies
- Vector-borne illnesses

TOXICOLOGY EMERGENCIES

- Acids and alkalis
- Carbon monoxide
- Cyanide
- Drug interactions (including alternative therapies)
- Overdose and ingestions
- Substance abuse
- Withdrawal syndrome

COMMUNICABLE DISEASES

- *C. Difficile*
- Childhood diseases
- Herpes zoster
- Mononucleosis
- Multidrug-resistant organisms
- Tuberculosis

PROFESSIONAL ISSUES

- Nurse
  - Critical Incident Stress Management
  - Ethical dilemmas
  - Evidence-based practice
  - Lifelong learning
  - Research
- Patient
  - Cultural considerations
  - Discharge planning
  - End-of-life issues
  - Forensic evidence collection
  - Pain management and procedural sedation
  - Patient safety
  - Patient satisfaction
  - Transfer and stabilization
  - Transitions of care
- System
  - Delegation of tasks to assistive personnel
  - Disaster management
  - Federal regulations
  - Patient consent for treatment
  - Performance improvement

- ○ Risk management
- ○ Symptom surveillance
- ○ Triage

Exam Administration

To register for the exam, you must first apply through the BCEN website (https://bcen.org/cen/apply-schedule). After your application is accepted, you will receive an email with instructions on how to register for the exam.

The CEN is administered at Pearson VUE testing centers around the nation. Plan to arrive at least **30 minutes before the exam**; if you arrive more than 15 minutes after the test starts, you will not be admitted. Bring **two forms of ID** and be prepared to be photographed and have a palm vein scan. Your primary ID must be government issued, include a recent photograph and signature, and match the name under which you registered to take the test. You secondary ID must include your name and signature or name and photograph. If you do not have proper ID, you will not be allowed to take the test.

You will not be allowed to bring any personal items into the testing room, such as calculators or phones. You may not bring pens, pencils, or scratch paper. Other prohibited items include hats, scarves, and coats. You may wear religious garments, however. Most testing centers provide lockers for valuables.

Exam Results

Once you have completed your test, the staff at the Pearson VUE testing center will give you a score report; you can also request to receive the report via email. The score report will include your raw score (the number of questions you answered correctly) for the whole test and for each content area.

The report will also include a pass/fail designation. The number of correct answers needed to pass the exam will vary slightly depending on the questions included in your version of the test (i.e., if you took a version of the test with harder questions, the passing score will be lower). For most test takers, **a passing score will be between 105 and 110** questions answered correctly.

If you do not pass the exam, you will be able to reapply and retake the test after 90 days.

Ascencia Test Prep

With health care fields such as nursing, pharmacy, emergency care, and physical therapy becoming the fastest-growing industries in the United States, individuals looking to enter the health care industry or rise in their field need high-quality, reliable resources. Ascencia Test Prep's study guides and test preparation materials are developed by credentialed industry professionals with years of experience in their respective fields. Ascencia recognizes that health care professionals nurture bodies and spirits, and save lives. Ascencia Test Prep's mission is to help health care workers grow.

ONE: DIAGNOSIS and MANAGEMENT

Cardiovascular Emergencies

management of NSTEMI

diagnosis of supraventricular tachycardia

- priority intervention: morphine, oxygen, nitrates, aspirin (MONA)
- other interventions: anticoagulant, calcium channel blockers, PCI
- monitoring: serial cardiac enzymes and ECG to monitor for heart damage

- ventricular rate between 150 – 300 bpm
- cannot identify P waves
- palpitations
- dizziness
- fatigue

atypical cardiac signs and symptoms
seen in women, patients with diabetes,
and geriatric patients

management of bradycardia

management of cardiogenic shock

- abdominal pain
- back pain
- heartburn/reflux

- oxygen
- stable patients: monitoring
- unstable patients: atropine (first-line), epinephrine (second-line)
- TCP if bradycardia is unresponsive to medication

- main goal is to identify and treat underlying cause (usually MI)
- medications to increase perfusion: antiplatelets, inotropes, vasopressors, nitroprusside
- other interventions: Fowler's position, IABP, PCI

diagnosis of unstable angina pectoris

diagnosis of cardiopulmonary arrest

diagnosis of aortic dissection

- sudden chest pain at rest, longer than 20 minutes, not relieved with meds or rest
- negative troponin and CK-MB
- ST depression

- no pulse
- no breathing, or agonal breathing
- no heart activity on FAST

- acute onset of severe sharp ripping, tearing pain in the chest or abdomen with possible radiation
- blood pressure difference of 20 mm Hg between left and right arms
- weak, unequal pulses
- imaging: CT scan, TEE

management of hypovolemic shock

diagnosis of NSTEMI

considerations for pregnancy in CPR

- volume resuscitation with isotonic crystalloid
- oxygen
- vasopressors
- blood products as indicated

- continuous chest pain with radiation
- positive troponin
- ST depression

- Displace the uterus to the left with wedge or pillow to avoid IVC compression.
- Chest compressions are higher on the chest.
- Mother is priority in resuscitation.

management of ventricular fibrillation

treatment of cardiopulmonary arrest

management of aortic dissection

- priority intervention: high-quality CPR and defibrillation
- epinephrine, amiodarone for shock-refractory V-fib

- immediate activation of code team
- immediate high-quality CPR
- Follow ACLS protocols for identified cardiac rhythm.

- blood pressure management (between 100 and 120 mm Hg systolic)
- beta blockers and nitroglycerin
- immediate surgical intervention

diagnosis of STEMI

diagnosis of ventricular fibrillation

management of endocarditis

- continuous chest pain with radiation
- positive troponin and CK-MB
- ST elevation

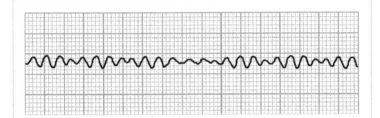

- often preceded by V-tach
- patient unresponsive
- lack of pulse, no breathing

- IV antibiotics (extended course)
- surgical intervention may be indicated for valve repair

diagnosis of pericarditis

diagnosis of ventricular tachycardia

diagnosis of bradycardia

- sudden, severe chest pain that increases with movement, lying flat, and inspiration
- Pain decreases when sitting up or leaning.
- pericardial friction rub
- elevated troponin
- possible ST elevation
- "water bottle" silhouette in CXR (pericardial effusion)

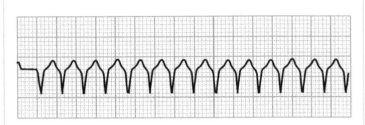

- dizziness or syncope
- palpitations
- chest pain

- HR < 60 bpm
- dizziness or syncope
- confusion
- hypotension

diagnosis of asystole

management of ventricular tachycardia

diagnosis of pulmonary hypertension

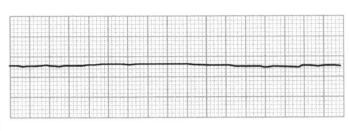

- no pulse
- no breathing, or agonal breathing

- no pulse: high-quality CPR and defibrillation
- pulse and stable: amiodarone, procainamide, sotalol
- pulse and unstable: synchronized cardioversion

- dyspnea
- JVD
- edema (lower extremity)
- ascites
- dizziness
- heart sounds: loud pulmonic valve sound, systolic murmur from tricuspid regurgitation, a gallop from ventricular failure

diagnosis of pulseless electrical activity

treatment of pulseless electrical activity

management of asystole

- organized rhythm on the monitor with no pulse
- no breathing, or agonal breathing

- immediate high-quality CPR
- epinephrine
- Identify underlying cause using Hs and Ts.

- immediate high-quality CPR
- epinephrine
- Identify underlying cause using Hs and Ts.

management of supraventricular
tachycardia

management of pericarditis

diagnosis of cardiogenic shock

- stable: vagal maneuvers (first-line), adenosine (second-line)
- unstable: synchronized cardioversion

- Allow patient to be in position of comfort.
- anti-inflammatory medications (e.g., ibuprofen or indomethacin)
- steroids or antibiotics as indicated
- pericardiocentesis for severe effusion

- hypotension and tachycardia
- oliguria
- dyspnea
- crackles
- diaphoresis
- pallor
- JVD
- cool and clammy skin

diagnosis of endocarditis

signs and symptoms of heart failure

diagnosis of hypertensive crisis

- chest pain
- flulike symptoms and fever
- Janeway lesions
- Osler's nodes
- joint pain
- dyspnea
- hematuria
- elevated WBC

- left sided (pulmonary s/s): dyspnea and cough, crackles, frothy sputum, left-sided S3 sound
- right sided (systemic circulatory s/s): edema, JVD, hepatomegaly, ascites, right-sided S3 sound
- BNP > 100 pg/mL

- BP > 180/110 mm Hg
- headache
- blurred vision
- dyspnea

management of hypertensive crisis

treatment of pulmonary hypertension

diagnosis of pericardial tamponade

- Decrease BP by no more than 25% within the first 2 hours.
- antihypertensive (e.g., labetalol, hydralazine, clonidine, metoprolol)

- oxygen
- vasodilators (sildenafil, tadalafil)
- diuretics
- anticoagulants

- Beck's triad (hypotension, JVD, muffled heart tones)
- pulsus paradoxus
- Kussmaul's sign
- chest pain

treatment of pericardial tamponade

diagnosis of deep vein thrombosis

treatment of deep vein thrombosis

- pericardiocentesis
- pericardial window
- inotropic drugs
- vasopressors

- pain localized to specific area (foot, ankle, calf, knee)
- unilateral edema, erythema, and warmth
- positive Homan's sign
- elevated D-dimer

- anticoagulants
- monitoring: frequent neurovascular checks of extremity and monitor for s/s of PE
- IVC filter may be placed to prevent PE.

management of unstable angina pectoris

diagnosis of hypovolemic shock

management of STEMI

- priority interventions: oxygen, 325 mg aspirin (or clopidogrel if aspirin contraindicated), and nitroglycerin
- other interventions: anticoagulant, calcium channel blockers, PCI
- monitoring: ECG to rule out development of STEMI

- hypotension and tachycardia
- tachypnea
- oliguria
- dizziness or confusion
- weakness
- diaphoresis
- cool, clammy skin

- priority intervention: morphine, oxygen, nitrates, aspirin (MONA)
- other interventions: anticoagulants, bivalirudin
- PCI or fibrinolytic therapy required

Respiratory Emergencies

diagnosis of pneumonia

management of croup

- productive cough
- pleuritic chest pain
- fever
- dyspnea
- hemoptysis
- abnormal sounds in the affected lung (decreased lung sounds, inspiratory crackles, dull percussion)
- increased WBC
- infiltrates on CXR

- oxygen
- cool mist therapy
- corticosteroids, dexamethasone, racemic epinephrine

diagnosis of bronchitis

diagnosis of asthma

management of pleural effusion

- nonproductive cough that evolves into a productive cough
- sore throat
- congestion
- fever
- chest discomfort
- fatigue

- wheezing
- frequent cough
- dyspnea
- tightness in chest
- decreased peak expiratory flow rate

- drain fluid
- diuretics

management of tension pneumothorax

diagnosis of COPD

diagnosis of bronchiolitis

immediate decompression via needle thoracostomy

- chronic productive cough
- dyspnea
- wheezing
- prolonged expiration
- hypoxemia

- Early presentation mimics common cold (rhinorrhea, congestion).
- Later symptoms indicate lower respiratory involvement (coughing, wheezing and crackles, increased respiratory effort, dyspnea).

management of bronchiolitis

management of COPD

management of asthma

- supportive treatment provided for symptoms (nasal suctioning, fluids, oxygen)
- pharmacological treatments for severe cases: bronchodilator, steroids, NSAIDS, nebulized albuterol

- acute exacerbation: bronchodilators, anticholinergics, cautious use of oxygen (titrated to SaO2 88 – 92% or PaO2 of 60 mm Hg)
- long-term management: expectorants, inhaled bronchodilators, inhaled corticosteroids

- acute exacerbation: inhaled bronchodilator (albuterol), corticosteroids, and oxygen
- Peak expiratory flow rate should increase after treatment with bronchodilator.
- long-term management: combination corticosteroid and bronchodilator

diagnosis of status asthmaticus

management of status asthmaticus

diagnosis of airway obstruction

severe, progressively worsening asthma event that does not respond to bronchodilator therapy

---

- inhaled bronchodilator (albuterol), corticosteroids, anti-cholinergic
- mechanical ventilation if asthma unresponsive to medication

---

- material visually observed in the airway
- dyspnea or gasping
- stridor
- excessive drooling in infants
- loss of consciousness and altered LOC
- respiratory arrest

management of airway obstruction

diagnosis of pleural effusion

diagnosis of tension pneumothorax

- suctioning of mouth and upper airway
- ET tube or cricothyrotomy if obstruction cannot be cleared

- dyspnea
- dullness on percussion
- asymmetrical chest expansion
- decreased breath sounds
- cough
- pleuritic chest pain

- sudden unilateral chest pain
- dyspnea
- tracheal deviation
- distended neck veins
- decreased breath sounds on affected side
- increased percussion noted on affected side

diagnosis of pulmonary edema

management of pulmonary edema

diagnosis of pulmonary embolism

- hemoptysis
- crackles
- coughing
- dyspnea
- hypoxia
- orthopnea

- oxygen
- Identify and treat underlying condition.

- pleuritic chest pain
- dyspnea and tachypnea
- cough
- hemoptysis
- hypotension and tachycardia
- positive D-dimer
- diagnosed via pulmonary angiography

management of pneumonia

diagnosis of croup

management of pulmonary embolism

- support adequate ventilation and oxygenation
- administer antibiotics

- barking cough
- hoarse cry
- high-pitched inspiratory stridor
- tachypnea

- IV anticoagulation (heparin)
- thrombolytic drugs
- supportive treatment (oxygen, analgesics, IV fluids, vasopressors)

management of bronchitis

diagnosis of tracheal rupture

- will spontaneously resolve without intervention
- supportive treatments for symptoms (fluids, antitussives, analgesics)

- hemoptysis
- dyspnea
- diffuse subcutaneous emphysema

Neurological Emergencies

diagnosis of amyotrophic lateral sclerosis (ALS)

management of multiple sclerosis (MS)

- progressive asymmetrical weakness (can affect both upper and lower extremities)
- difficulty swallowing or eating
- difficulty walking
- muscle cramps
- difficulty speaking or slurred speech

acute exacerbation: corticosteroids, baclofen (Lioresal), gabapentin (Neurontin)

diagnosis of ischemic stroke

management of myasthenia gravis (MG)

diagnosis of Guillain-Barré syndrome

- facial drooping, usually on one side
- numbness, paralysis, or weakness on one side of the body
- slurred speech or inability to speak
- confusion
- vision changes
- dizziness or loss of balance control
- sudden onset of severe headache
- arm drift

- myasthenic crisis: IV fluids, IV immunoglobulin, anticholinesterase
- cholinergic crisis: mechanical ventilation, atropine, discontinue anticholinesterase

---

- neuropathy and weakness ascending from lower extremities and advancing symmetrically upward
- dyspnea
- paresthesia in extremities
- absent or diminished deep tendon reflexes
- autonomic dysfunction (heart block, bradycardia, hypotension)

management of neurogenic shock

diagnosis of autonomic dysreflexia

management of increased intracranial
pressure

- IV fluids (first-line), vasopressors (second-line) for hypotension
- atropine for bradycardia

- flushing and sweating above the level of injury
- cold, clammy skin below the level of injury
- bradycardia
- sudden, severe headache
- hypertension

---

reduce pressure: IV mannitol, hypertonic saline, sedatives, shunt

diagnosis of myasthenic crisis

diagnosis of epidural hematoma

management of meningitis

- dyspnea, aspiration, or respiratory failure in patients with myasthenia gravis (usually requires mechanical ventilation)
- bulbar weakness (dysphagia, absent gag reflex)

- unconsciousness followed by a coherent "normal" interval and subsequent rapid deterioration
- confusion
- dizziness
- anisocoria
- headache
- nausea and vomiting
- one-sided oculomotor paralysis
- contralateral hemiplegia

- standard and droplet isolation precautions
- corticosteroids
- treatment for bacterial or viral infection

diagnosis of status epilepticus

diagnosis of anterior spinal cord syndrome

diagnosis of increased intracranial pressure

- seizure activity lasting longer than 5 minutes
- repeat seizures with no regaining of consciousness between

- complete motor loss below the lesion
- loss of sensation of pain and temperature below the lesion
- lower extremities affected more than upper extremities

- ICP > 20 mm Hg
- headache
- nausea and vomiting
- decreased LOC
- diplopia or pupils unreactive to light
- dyspnea
- separation of bony plates and bulging fontanel in children

diagnosis of Brown-Séquard syndrome

diagnosis of cauda equina syndrome

management of status epilepticus

- ipsilateral motor loss below the lesion
- contralateral loss of sensation of pain and temperature

- sensory loss in the lower extremities
- bowel and bladder dysfunction
- severe lower back pain

- first-line treatment: benzodiazepines
- protect patient from injury and secure airway

diagnosis of central cord syndrome

management of Guillain-Barré syndrome

diagnosis of neurogenic shock

- greater motor function loss in the upper extremities than in the lower extremities
- weakness
- paresthesia in upper extremities
- greater deficits in hands

- first-line treatment for acute exacerbation: IV immuno-globulins
- other interventions: plasmapheresis, mechanical ventilation

---

- hemodynamic triad (rapid onset of hypotension, bradycardia, and hypothermia)
- skin warm, flushed, and dry
- wide pulse pressure
- priapism

management of autonomic dysreflexia

diagnosis of hemorrhagic stroke

diagnosis of meningitis

- Have patient empty the bladder and bowel.
- Remove tight clothing.
- Administer antihypertensives.

- severe, sudden headache
- sudden onset of weakness
- difficulty speaking and walking
- lethargy, altered LOC, or coma

- stiff neck (extremely painful to move the neck forward)
- severe headache
- fever
- diagnosed via CSF analysis

management of ischemic stroke

diagnosis of transient ischemic attack

diagnosis of multiple sclerosis (MS)

- priority intervention is CT scan to assess for hemorrhage
- If CT scan is negative for hemorrhage, administer tPA (within 4.5 hours of onset of symptoms).

---

s/s of ischemic stroke lasting < 1 hour

- paresthesia
- weakness of at least one extremity
- visual disturbances
- gait disturbance
- urinary incontinence
- vertigo
- increased deep tendon reflexes
- positive Babinski sign

diagnosis of diffuse axonal injury

management of hemorrhagic stroke

- retinal hemorrhages (seen with shaken-baby syndrome)
- decreased or complete loss of consciousness
- decorticate or decerebrate posturing
- hypertension
- diaphoresis
- hyperthermia
- amnesia or confusion

- secure patient's airway
- monitor and treat increased ICP

Gastrointestinal Emergencies

diagnosis of upper GI bleed

management of esophageal varices

- upper abdominal pain
- hematemesis
- melena
- coffee-ground emesis
- hematochezia (if hemorrhaging)
- s/s of hypovolemia (after significant blood loss)

- manage hemodynamic status: IV fluids, blood products, and management of coagulopathies
- medications to constrict vasculature: vasopressin, octreotides (e.g., Sandostatin), and beta blockers

management of cirrhosis

diagnosis of lower gastric bleeding

diagnosis of gastroenteritis

- vitamin K, FFP, and platelets as needed
- lactulose for elevated ammonia levels
- thiamine and folic acid replacement
- avoid NSAIDs
- patient education on alcohol cessation or weight loss

- abdominal pain
- hematochezia
- melena
- s/s of hypovolemia

- nausea and vomiting
- diarrhea
- diffuse and cramping abdominal pain
- fever
- dehydration

management of appendicitis

diagnosis of cholecystitis

management of pancreatitis

- Keep patient NPO and prepare for surgery.
- analgesics, antiemetics, antibiotics

- RUQ pain, which can radiate to back or right shoulder (common after eating high-fat meal)
- colicky pain
- positive Murphy's sign
- nausea, vomiting, or anorexia
- flatulence
- jaundice (if obstruction is significant)
- diagnosed via CT scan

- control pain (avoid morphine)
- IV fluid resuscitation
- keep patient NPO
- monitoring: ARDS, atelectasis, retroperitoneal bleeding

diagnosis of bowel obstruction

management of gastroenteritis

diagnosis of bowel infarction

- abdominal pain, typically described as cramping and colicky
- distended and firm abdomen
- unable to pass flatus
- high-pitched bowel sounds (early); absent bowel sounds (late)
- tympanic percussion
- nausea, vomiting, or diarrhea

- IV fluid resuscitation and electrolyte replacement
- antiemetics, anticholinergics
- discharge: PO challenge, teach BRAT diet

- abdominal pain, cramping, and distension
- nausea, vomiting, or diarrhea
- hematochezia
- fever

diagnosis of intussusception

diagnosis of pyloric stenosis

diagnosis of appendicitis

- red currant jelly–like stool
- sausage-shaped abdominal mass
- colicky pain
- inconsolable crying
- absence of stools

- projectile vomiting, especially after eating
- an olive-shaped mass in the RUQ
- visible peristalsis
- frequent hunger
- poor weight gain

- dull, steady periumbilical pain
- RLQ pain that worsens with movement
- pain in RLQ at McBurney's point
- positive Rovsing's sign
- positive psoas sign
- fever
- rebound tenderness
- abdominal rigidity
- diagnosed via CT scan

diagnosis of diverticulitis

management of bowel infarction

diagnosis of pancreatitis

- LLQ abdominal pain and distention
- rebound tenderness
- nausea, vomiting, or anorexia
- fever
- hematochezia

- analgesics, antiemetics
- keep patient NPO
- IV fluid resuscitation
- NG tube for gastric decompression

- dull and steady pain, usually in LUQ
- guarding
- decreased bowel sounds
- steatorrhea
- Cullen's sign
- Grey-Turner's sign
- nausea, vomiting, or anorexia
- elevated amylase and lipase

management of cholecystitis

diagnosis of cirrhosis

management of bowel obstruction

- analgesics, antiemetics
- ERCP to remove stones in bile duct
- discharge: teach patient to avoid high-fat foods

- bleeding and bruising easily
- pruritus
- jaundice
- ascites
- spiderlike angiomas
- asterixis
- elevated AST, ALT, bilirubin, and ammonia
- decreased protein, albumin, and fibrinogen
- decreased WBCs, HgB, Hct, and platelets
- longer PT and PTT, and increased INR

- analgesics, antiemetics
- keep patient NPO
- IV fluid resuscitation
- NG tube for gastric decompression

management of diverticulitis

management of intussusception

- antibiotics
- IV fluid resuscitation and electrolyte replacement
- liquid diet
- discharge teaching: stool softeners, low-fiber diet until the inflammation is reduced, then a high-fiber diet to prevent straining

- keep patient NPO
- enema, surgery

Genitourinary and Gynecologic Emergencies

diagnosis of pyelonephritis

management of foreign bodies in the gynecological system

- clinical triad (fever, nausea/vomiting, and costovertebral pain)
- cloudy, dark, foul-smelling urine
- hematuria
- dysuria
- suprapubic, cervical, or uterine tenderness

- speculum and forceps to remove object in vagina
- warm water lavage of the vagina for objects that can be easily dislodged
- sedation and/or anesthesia for objects that cannot be removed without pain or further injury

diagnosis of epididymitis

management of genital herpes

management of renal calculi

- pain posterior to testes (gradual onset, can radiate to lower abdomen)
- s/s of UTI
- positive Prehn sign
- edema and tenderness in testes

antivirals (acyclovir, famciclovir [Famvir], valacyclovir [Valtrex])

- analgesics, alpha blockers
- Small stones (< 5 mm) will pass spontaneously.
- large stones removed via ESWL

diagnosis of pelvic inflammatory disease (PID)

management of prostatitis

diagnosis of testicular torsion

- abdominal or low back pain
- cervical, uterine, or adnexal tenderness
- vaginal discharge
- pleuritic URQ pain or right scapular pain (Fitz-Hugh–Curtis syndrome)
- postcoital bleeding or metrorrhagia
- temperature > 38°C (100.4°F)

---

antibiotics, NSAIDs

- sudden, severe unilateral scrotal pain
- high-riding testicle
- absent cremasteric reflex
- s/s of inflammation in scrotal skin

management of pyelonephritis

management of penile fracture

diagnosis of renal calculi

- IV fluid resuscitation (D5W)
- antibiotics, antipyretics, analgesics, antiemetics

- IV fluids
- pain management (analgesics, cold compress, pressure dressing)
- prepare patient for surgery

- severe, sudden, and sharp flank pain (may radiate to abdomen or groin)
- dysuria
- hematuria
- urine frequency and urgency
- fever and chills

management of epididymitis

management of pelvic inflammatory disease (PID)

diagnosis of genital herpes

- antibiotics
- pain management (analgesics, ice packs, scrotal support or elevation)
- surgery for severe infection (epididymectomy)

antibiotics, analgesics

- prodrome of itching, burning, or tingling at infection site
- vesicles on genitalia, perineum, or buttocks
- primary infection with fever and adenopathy

diagnosis of prostatitis

management of testicular torsion

diagnosis of penile fracture

- frequent, urgent urination
- dysuria
- urinary retention
- suprapubic or perineal pain (may occur in external genitals or low back)

- analgesics
- Prepare patient for immediate surgery.

- popping, snapping, or cracking noise
- sudden detumescence
- may present with pain
- penile deformity ("eggplant" or "aubergine sign")
- ecchymosis and edema
- hematuria

Obstetrical Emergencies

management of ectopic pregnancy

diagnosis of hyperemesis gravidarum

- RhoGAM if mother is Rh negative
- hemodynamically unstable patients: surgery
- hemodynamically stable patients: OB referral for surgery or treatment with methotrexate

- persistent vomiting (> 3 times per day)
- weight loss of > 5 pounds or > 5% of body weight
- s/s of hypovolemia

management of umbilical cord prolapse

diagnosis of ectopic pregnancy

indications for neonatal resuscitation

- Apply saline-soaked sterile gauze to exposed umbilical cord.
- Elevate presenting part of fetus manually or through positioning.
- Place patient in Trendelenburg or knee-chest position.
- Retrofill bladder.

- s/s of pregnancy
- vaginal bleeding
- abdominal pain
- s/s of hemorrhage (if fallopian tube ruptures)

- respiratory intervention: HR < 100 bpm
- compressions: HR < 60 bpm
- absence of spontaneous breath or vigorous cry
- airway obstruction (nares and/or trachea)
- cyanosis
- poor muscle tone

management of preeclampsia

diagnosis of abruptio placentae

management of hyperemesis gravidarum

- antihypertensives
- magnesium (prevents seizures)
- admit to OB

- vaginal bleeding (light to heavy)
- contractions
- firm uterus
- abdominal or back pain (depending on location of placenta)
- s/s of hemorrhage

- IV fluid resuscitation
- replace electrolytes, vitamins, and minerals
- antiemetics
- patient education: BRAT diet, avoiding triggers

diagnosis of eclampsia

management of postpartum hemorrhage

diagnosis of postpartum infection

- signs and symptoms of preeclampsia
- tonic-clonic seizures

- IV fluid resuscitation
- blood products as needed
- tranexamic acid

- temperature of ≥ 38°C (100.4°F) (on more than 2 days or maintained over 24 hours postpartum)
- endometritis: uterine tenderness and midline lower abdominal pain
- surgical incision infection: erythema and inflammation at incision
- mastitis: erythema and tenderness in breast

management of abruptio placentae

diagnosis of placenta previa

diagnosis of spontaneous abortion

- IV fluids
- RhoGAM if mother is Rh negative
- monitoring: fetal heart rate monitoring, monitor mother for hemodynamic instability
- admit to OB

asymptomatic or painless vaginal bleeding

- vaginal bleeding
- passage of fetal tissue
- radiating pelvic pain
- s/s of cessation of pregnancy
- s/s of infection with septic abortion

management of postpartum infection

diagnosis of preeclampsia

- endometritis and UTI: antibiotics
- surgical incision: drain, irrigate, and debride wound
- mastitis: antibiotics, empty breast of milk

- may occur intra- or postpartum
- hypertension (systolic BP > 140 mm Hg or diastolic BP > 90 mm Hg)
- facial edema
- rapid weight gain (> 5 pounds a week)
- headache
- epigastric pain
- pitting edema
- proteinuria

Psychosocial Emergencies

management of abuse and neglect

signs and symptoms of schizophrenia

- Protected populations (including pediatric and geriatric patients) require obligatory reporting of suspected abuse and neglect.
- The priority treatment of the abused or neglected patient should focus on physical injuries.

- positive
  - delusions and hallucinations
  - disorganized speech
  - odd or confusing behavior
- negative
  - social withdrawal
  - paranoia
  - flattened affect
  - poverty of speech

protocols for restraint use

management of anxiety and panic

signs and symptoms of bipolar disorder

- should be used conservatively
- only for patients whose behavior cannot be controlled through less restrictive measures
- require frequent assessment (every 5 – 15 minutes depending on policy)
- Check vitals, assess pain, assess circulation and skin integrity of all restrained extremities, and address restroom needs.
- should be removed as soon as they are deemed unnecessary for patient and staff safety

- non-pharmacological interventions: calming environment, rhythmic breathing, social support
- pharmacological interventions: benzodiazepines, antihistamines (hydroxyzine)

- manic behavior:
  - feelings of elation
  - high levels of energy and increased activity
  - difficulty sleeping; may not sleep for several days
  - increased rate of speech
  - engaging in high-risk activities
- depressive behavior:
  - deep or intense feelings of sadness
  - decreased energy levels and decreased activity
  - sleep and appetite disturbances
  - suicidal ideation or focus on death
  - feelings of anxiety or worry

management of suicidal ideation

signs and symptoms of abuse
and neglect

management of bipolar disorder

- Screen for suicidal ideation in all patients. (Assess for admission based on the severity of suicidal ideation or behavior.)
- Secure all weapons in the patient's possession.
- Secure a contract of safety with the patient.
- Create an environment of safety for the patient.
- Establish 1:1 watch or line-of-sight supervision for the patient.

- unexplained injuries
- fractures or bruising at different stages of healing
- poor hygiene
- weight loss or gain
- alopecia from hair pulling or lack of repositioning
- severe mood swings or changes
- agitation, depression, or withdrawal
- sleep disturbance

---

acute exacerbations: mood stabilizers, atypical antipsychotics, antipsychotics and antidepressants (usually used long-term)

Medical Emergencies

management of disseminated intravascular coagulopathy (DIC)

management of acute adrenal crisis (Addisonian crisis)

- IV fluid resuscitation
- vasopressors
- transfusion of blood products (FFP, PRBCs, platelets, or cryoprecipitate)
- heparin for chronic DIC

- Treatment is based on clinical appearance and is not delayed pending diagnostic test results.
- IV fluid resuscitation
- IV corticosteroids
- oxygen

management of hypokalemia

diagnosis of hyponatremia

diagnosis of sepsis

potassium (PO or IV)

- low sodium (< 135 mEq/L)
- weakness and lethargy
- nausea
- headache
- dizziness
- cerebral edema
- seizures or coma

- 2 or more signs or symptoms of SIRS, plus suspected or confirmed infection
- serum lactate > 2 mmol/L

management of thyrotoxic crisis

management of hyperkalemia

diagnosis of diabetes insipidus

- treatment based on clinical appearance and not delayed pending thyroid study results
- thyroid hormone–inhibiting medications (PTU or MMI), corticosteroids, iodine, beta blockers, digoxin
- antipyretics, other cooling measures
- oxygen
- IV fluids

- calcium gluconate
- IV insulin and D50
- loop diuretics (furosemide)
- sodium polystyrene sulfonate (Kayexalate)
- sodium bicarbonate
- beta 2 agonists (albuterol)
- hypertonic IV solution (3% normal saline)
- dialysis
- monitoring: ECG

- polydipsia
- polyuria
- dehydration
- low urine osmolality (< 300 mOsm/kg)
- low urine specific gravity (1.001 – 1.005)
- high serum Na+ (> 145 mEq/L)
- high serum osmolality

diagnosis of hypermagnesemia

management of hyponatremia

diagnosis of allergic reaction

- high magnesium (> 2.5 mEq/L)
- dysrhythmias or cardiac arrest:
  - prolonged PR interval
  - wide QRS complex
  - peaked T waves
- bradycardia, hypotension, and respiratory depression
- altered mental status, lethargy, or coma

- Sodium replacement (PO or IV): Do not exceed 12 mEq/L in a 24-hour period.
- Restrict fluid intake and monitor I/O.

- topical dermatitis
- urticaria (hives)
- rhinorrhea and sneezing
- itchy eyes, skin, nose, or mouth
- circumoral tingling or pallor
- mild nausea or abdominal discomfort

management of hypomagnesemia

diagnosis of anaphylactic shock

diagnosis of hypernatremia

- magnesium (PO or IV)
- monitoring: swallowing, seizures, ECG

- respiratory distress
- throat tightness
- edema in face, lips, or tongue
- skin pallor or flushing
- hypotension
- weak thread pulse
- syncope or presyncope

- high sodium (> 145 mEq/L)
- tachycardia
- elevated body temperature
- hyperreflexia, including twitching
- polydipsia
- lethargy or decreased LOC
- seizures or coma

management of anaphylactic reactions

management of hypermagnesemia

diagnosis of acute adrenal crisis
(Addisonian crisis)

epinephrine (IM injection)

- calcium gluconate
- loop diuretics
- isotonic IV solutions (lactated Ringer's or 0.9% normal saline)
- dialysis

- s/s of hypovolemic shock
- hyperpigmentation
- nausea, vomiting, and abdominal pain
- history of weight loss, anorexia, and craving for salt
- decreased serum cortisol
- hyperkalemia or hyponatremia

diagnosis of hypomagnesemia

management of allergic reaction

management of diabetes insipidus

- low magnesium (< 1.3 mEq/L)
- dysrhythmias:
  - torsades de pointes
  - flat or inverted T waves
  - ST depression
  - prolonged PR interval
  - widened QRS complex
- tetany (Chvostek sign, Trousseau sign)
- hyperreflexia
- seizures

H1 antihistamines, H2 antihistamines, glucocorticoid, broncho-dilator, topical antihistamines

- vasopressin
- IV fluid resuscitation
- treat electrolyte imbalances
- monitoring: I/O, ECG

diagnosis of hypoglycemia

diagnosis of thyrotoxic crisis

diagnosis of hyperkalemia

- serum glucose < 70 mg/dL
- shakes/tremors
- tachycardia
- confusion, altered LOC, dizziness, or syncope
- cold, clammy skin
- hunger
- blurred vision
- circumoral tingling
- seizures

- hyperpyrexia
- tachycardia
- respiratory distress
- altered mental status
- nausea, vomiting, or diarrhea
- ophthalmopathy
- stupor or coma

- high potassium (> 5.0 mEq/L)
- dysrhythmias or cardiac arrest:
  - tall, peaked T waves
  - wide QRS complex
  - absent P waves
  - ST depression
- abdominal cramping and diarrhea
- muscle weakness

diagnosis of disseminated intravascular coagulopathy (DIC)

management of hypoglycemia

diagnosis of renal failure

- s/s of bleeding (e.g., spontaneous hemorrhage, petechiae)
- s/s of thromboembolic event (e.g., PE, DVT)
- decreased platelets (moderate to severe)
- prolonged PT and PTT
- decreased fibrinogen
- severely elevated D-dimer and FSP

- conscious patient: 15 – 30 grams of carbohydrates PO
- unconscious or unable to ingest carbohydrates PO: IM glucagon, D50 IV

- oliguria or anuria
- increased creatinine and BUN
- elevated BUN: creatinine ratio
- low urine Na+
- increased urine osmolality and specific gravity

criteria for SIRS

diagnosis of hypokalemia

management of renal failure

- temperature > 38.3°C (101°F) or < 36°C (96.9°F)
- HR > 90 bpm
- RR > 20 per minute
- $PaCO_2$ < 32 mm Hg
- WBC > 12,000/mm3 or < 4,000/mm3 or > 10% bands

- low potassium (< 3.5 mEq/L)
- muscle weakness and cramps
- hypotension
- altered mental status
- hypoactive reflexes
- dysrhythmias (V-tach, V-fib, AV block, bradycardia)

- Manage fluid volume.
  - IV fluids for hypovolemic patients
  - loop diuretics for hypervolemic patients
  - daily weights and strict I/O
- Correct electrolyte imbalances.
- bicarbonate for metabolic acidosis

management of hypernatremia

management of sepsis

- restrict dietary sodium
- increase fluid intake (D5W or other hypotonic IV solutions)
- diuretics

- oxygen
- IV fluids
- broad-spectrum antibiotics
- vasopressor for hypotension

Maxillofacial Emergencies

management of labyrinthitis

diagnosis of Ménière's disease

- corticosteroids
- antibiotics or antivirals
- treat symptoms: antihistamines, antiemetics, benzodiaze-pines, meclizine

- attacks can occur frequently (several times a day) or infrequently (years apart)
- classic triad of symptoms: fluctuations in hearing/ hearing loss, tinnitus, vertigo

diagnosis of dental abscess

management of Bell's palsy

diagnosis of trigeminal neuralgia

- orofacial edema
- halitosis
- visible pus or exudate
- taste of pus or exudate in mouth
- fever

- corticosteroids
- oral glycerin swabs for dry mouth; Yankauer suction for excess saliva
- patch on affected eye if diminished blink reflex to limit risk for corneal abrasion

---

- characteristic unilateral pain along branches of the fifth cranial nerve
- abrupt onset and ending of pain lasting several minutes to several days
- trigger points associated with onset of pain
- facial muscle contractions causing eye to close and mouth to twitch on affected side

management of peritonsillar abscess

diagnosis of Ludwig's angina

management of otitis

- ABCs: secure airway, suction as needed
- incise and drain
- antibiotics, analgesics, corticosteroids

- tongue enlargement and protrusion
- sublingual pain and tenderness
- compromised breathing
- drooling and difficulty swallowing
- neck pain, edema, and erythema
- fever and chills

- usually heal spontaneously
- antibiotics (oral or drops if tympanic membrane is ruptured)
- analgesics

diagnosis of mastoiditis

diagnosis of peritonsillar abscess

management of trigeminal neuralgia

- otitis media
- tympanic membrane rupture
- fever
- papilledema
- erythema and edema over mastoid process

- visible abscess on soft palate
- severe sore throat
- enlarged lymph nodes
- trismus
- dysphagia or drooling
- halitosis

---

anti-seizure medications (carbamazepine [Tegretol], gabapentin [Neurontin], baclofen [Lioresal])

diagnosis of ruptured tympanic membrane

management of Ludwig's angina

diagnosis of temporomandibular joint dislocation

- severe pain upon rupture, which quickly subsides
- fluid drainage (can be clear, purulent, or sanguineous)
- hearing loss or reduction
- tinnitus
- vertigo with nausea and vomiting
- whistling sound or crepitus when blowing nose

- ABCs are the priority: ET tube or tracheotomy, oxygen.
- IV antibiotics
- incise and drain

- palpable displacement of joint
- jaw pain
- malocclusion
- speech difficulties
- dysphagia or drooling
- trismus

management of Ménière's disease

diagnosis of otitis

management of temporomandibular joint dislocation

- diuretics (non-potassium-sparing)
- intratympanic gentamicin or steroids (injected by ENT)
- treat symptoms: antihistamines, antiemetics, benzodiaze-pines, meclizine
- reduced sodium diet

- otalgia
- otorrhea
- tugging on ear
- loss of balance
- s/s of infection

- ABCs: secure airway
- manual or surgical reduction

diagnosis of labyrinthitis

management of dental abscess

diagnosis of Bell's palsy

- dizziness or vertigo
- loss of balance and equilibrium
- tinnitus or hearing loss
- fever
- irritability or lethargy in children
- nausea and vomiting

- incise and drain
- antibiotics, analgesics

- mild to total unilateral paralysis of facial muscles
- characteristic facial droop
- asymmetrical facial features and smile
- painful sensations on affected side
- difficulty speaking
- dysphagia

management of mastoiditis

antibiotics, analgesics

Ocular Emergencies

management of foreign bodies in the ocular region

diagnosis of glaucoma

- Irrigate with normal saline or eye wash solution.
- Morgan Lens may be used for extraocular foreign bodies, or if sensation of foreign body is present but foreign body is not visible.
- Remove foreign body using cotton-tipped applicator, metal spud, or 25-gauge needle (extraocular only).
- topical anesthetic (caines) and antibiotic

- abrupt onset of pain
- visual changes (blurry, cloudy, or halos of light)
- headache
- erythema
- corneal edema with clouding
- fixed pupil, mid-dilated (5 – 6 mm)

management of conjunctivitis

diagnosis of hyphema

diagnosis of retinal artery occlusion

- topical antibiotics, steroids
- ophthalmic lubricating solution
- Discharge teaching: Do not wear contact lenses until infection has resolved, do not share makeup or facecloths, wash hands frequently.

- visible accumulation of blood between cornea and iris
- decreased visual acuity
- pain

---

unilateral, sudden, painless loss of vision

diagnosis of retinal detachment

management of glaucoma

diagnosis of conjunctivitis

- painless gradual onset of visual changes (reduction in peripheral vision and curtain-like shadow)
- photopsia
- sudden or gradual increase of multiple floaters

- topical miotic ophthalmic drops to constrict pupil (pilocarpine), topical beta blockers, alpha-adrenergic agents (clonidine)
- IV acetazolamide and mannitol

- burning or itching sensation
- increased lacrimation (clear or yellow)
- edema of palpebra
- sensation of foreign body or grit
- typically no decrease in visual acuity

management of hyphema

management of retinal detachment

management of retinal artery occlusion

- elevate head of bed ≥ 45 degrees
- bed rest
- topical corticosteroids, cycloplegics, beta blockers, alpha-adrenergic agents (clonidine)
- IV acetazolamide, mannitol

bed rest and referral to ophthalmology

- topical beta blockers
- IV acetazolamide, mannitol, methylprednisolone
- ocular massage

Orthopedic Injuries

diagnosis of Achilles tendon rupture

management of amputation

- pain, edema, and tenderness in ankle
- decreased strength
- hearing or feeling a pop on occurrence
- unable to flex foot or push off on toes when walking

- ABCs
- Preserve detached limb.
- Gently replace attached tissue and maintain normal positioning.
- IV fluids and blood products as needed

management of costochondritis

types of blast injuries

diagnosis of compartment syndrome

- spontaneous resolves
- treatment of symptoms: rest, heat or ice, anti-inflammatories

---

- primary injuries: caused by wave of increased pressure
  - blast lung injuries (BLI) clinical triad: apnea, hypotension, bradycardia
  - ruptured tympanic membrane
- secondary injuries: caused by debris (e.g., lacerations, fractures, crush injuries)

- the 6 P's
  - pain (not proportional to injury)
  - pallor
  - pulselessness
  - paresthesia
  - paralysis
  - poikilothermia
- decreased urine output
- tissue tight on palpation
- tight, shiny skin

management of Achilles tendon rupture

management of compartment syndrome

diagnosis of costochondritis

- ice and analgesics
- stabilize ankle flexed downward (walking boot or cast)

- analgesics, IV fluids
- definitive treatment is surgery (fasciotomy)

- tenderness on palpation of rib joints
- sharp pain at chest wall (may radiate to abdomen or back)
- rib pain increases with deep breathing and movement of the trunk
- can cause breathing problems

Wounds

management of pressure ulcers

diagnosis of stage 4 pressure ulcer

- Measures to prevent pressure ulcers include systematic position changes and positioning devices.
- Stage 1: Preventive measures include repositioning and transparent film.
- Stage 2: Dress wound to maintain moist environment.
- Stages 3 and 4: Debride necrotic tissues (surgical or hydrogel dressing).
- Other interventions include NPWT and topical antibiotics.

- full-thickness tissue loss extending through the fascia
- visibly exposed bone, tendons, and muscle
- slough and eschar

management of abrasions

diagnosis of abscess

management of avulsions

- irrigate wound and clean with saline solution or mild soap and water
- topical anesthetic, antibiotic
- cover using clean, moist dressing (nonstick/non-adherent dressing)

- raised focal area of induration (hardened mass)
- pustule "head"
- erythema of overlying epidermis
- warm and tender to touch
- spongy/fluid-filled
- nonmobile and non-firm to palpation

- Control bleeding.
- Use topical or local anesthetic (e.g., lidocaine [Xylocaine]).
  - Avoid using anesthetic containing epinephrine for avulsions of face, phalanges, or male genitalia.
- Debride and irrigate wound.
- Cover wound with absorbent, non-adhering bandage or dressing.
- Ice and elevate.

diagnosis of pilonidal cyst

diagnosis of stage 1 pressure ulcer

management of abscess

- palpable abscess or "bump" at base of tailbone or upper cleft of buttocks
- pain with palpation
- inability to sit comfortably

- intact skin
- area of localized erythema in patients with light-pigmented skin
- area of localized blue, purple, or dark red hue in patients with dark-pigmented skin
- non-blanchable

- incise and drain (needle aspiration)
- wound may be packed for wicking effect
- antibiotics

Environmental Emergencies

diagnosis of superficial
(first degree) burn

diagnosis of deep partial-thickness burn

- affects only the epidermis
- reddened area

- affects epidermis and dermis
- color is white or red
- does not blanch
- blisters

management of Lyme disease

diagnosis of rabies

management of food poisoning

oral or IV antibiotics (amoxicillin, doxycycline, ceftriaxone)

- Initial symptoms are nonspecific (fever, headache).
- encephalitis (confusion, agitation, hallucinations)
- excessive salivation
- hydrophobia
- ascending paralysis that progresses to quadriplegia

- supportive treatment: oral or IV hydration, electrolyte replacement
- Antibiotics are not usually given for a diagnosis of food poisoning.

management of hypothermia

management of heat stroke

diagnosis of Lyme disease

- The first line of treatment is to prevent further heat loss: Remove wet or cold clothing, insulate patient.
- Mild hypothermia: Passively rewarm patients at a rate of 1°C per hour with an insulated blanket and warmed oral fluids.
- Severe hypothermia: Patients should be treated with active core warming via heated oxygen (40°C – 45°C [104°F – 113°F]) and IV fluids (0°C – 42°C [104°F – 107.6°F]).

- Cooling methods include evaporative cooling, convective cooling, and immersion in cold water.
- Treat shivering during cooling to minimize vasoconstriction (benzodiazepines, chlorpromazine [Thorazine]).

- first stage (early localized stage, 3 – 30 days post-bite): erythema migrans (bull's-eye rash)
- second stage (early disseminated stage, several weeks): nonspecific flulike symptoms
- late stage (months to years after infection if left untreated): characterized by arthritis and periods of fatigue and low-grade fever

IV fluid management of burns

diagnosis of heat stroke

management of rabies

- IV lactated Ringer's per Parkland formula:
- 4 ml × TBSA (%) × body weight (kg)
- Give 50% in first 8 hours; then 50% in next 16 hours.
- Formula time starts at the time the burn happens.
- Expected urine output is 0.5 ml/kg/hr in adults and 0.5 – 1.0 ml/kg/hr in children < 30 kg.

- temperature > 104°F (40°C)
- dysfunction of the CNS (confusion, delirium, seizure)
- tachycardia and tachypnea

- Clean the wound with soap and water or BZK wipes.
- Administer rabies vaccine and rabies immune globulin (RIG).
- After exposure, vaccines are given: 1.0 ml IM on days 0, 3, 7, and 14.
- Once rabies has developed, there is no curative treatment.

Toxicology Emergencies

diagnosis of delirium tremens

management of carbon monoxide poisoning

- 72 – 96 hours after last drink
- fluctuation changes in cognition
- hallucinations
- tachycardia and hypertension
- fever

- 100% oxygen through non-rebreather
- Hyperbaric oxygen may be used to treat patients with severe symptoms.

management of opioid withdrawal

signs and symptoms of
carbon monoxide poisoning

signs and symptoms of opioid
withdrawal

- benzodiazepines, antiemetics, clonidine, antidiarrheals
- methadone or buprenorphine to relieve symptoms

- headache
- altered LOC
- dizziness or syncope
- confusion
- visual disturbances
- dyspnea on exertion
- vomiting
- muscle weakness and cramps
- seizure

- drug craving
- nausea, vomiting, and diarrhea
- abdominal cramping
- dysphoria and anxiety
- yawning, rhinorrhea, and lacrimation
- mydriasis
- piloerection
- sweating
- muscle pain and twitching
- tachycardia, tachypnea, and hypertension

management of alcohol withdrawal

- IV fluid resuscitation and electrolyte imbalances
- Treat for vitamin deficiencies and malnutrition (glucose, thiamine, folate).
- benzodiazepines for agitation and seizures
- drug "cocktail" for drug-resistant DTs includes lorazepam, diazepam, and midazolam (Versed) or propofol

Communicable Diseases

diagnosis of C. *difficile*

management of diphtheria

- foul-smelling diarrhea 5 – 10 days after start of antibiotic (sometimes bloody)
- abdominal pain

- pharyngeal infection: diphtheria antitoxin, antibiotics
- Skin infection: Clean with soap and water, antibiotics.
- Diphtheria vaccination is given after recovery.
- monitoring: ECGs for myocarditis
- antibiotics and vaccinations for close contacts

signs and symptoms of mumps

management of pertussis

diagnosis of measles

- general s/s of fever
- 12 – 24 hours after symptoms begin:
  - salivary gland edema
  - parotitis
  - pain when chewing or swallowing
  - tongue and submandibular glands may swell

- antibiotics (erythromycin, azithromycin [Zithromax])
- supportive care: suctioning in infants, intubation

- fever
- respiratory s/s (cough, runny nose)
- sore throat
- Koplik spots
- cephalocaudal rash behind ears
- photophobia
- positive test for measles-specific immunoglobulin M (IgM)

management of mononucleosis

management of *C. difficile*

management of tuberculosis

- supportive care for symptoms: corticosteroids, fluids
- Administer corticosteroids for severe symptoms, such as airway obstruction.
- Teach patient to rest and avoid heavy activity until splenomegaly resolves.

- For antibiotic-induced *C. diff.*, stop current use of antibiotics if possible.
- Treat with metronidazole (Flagyl), vancomycin (Vancocin), or fidaxomicin (Dificid).

- 2 month treatment with isoniazid (INH), rifampin (RIF), pyrazinamide (PZA), and ethambutol (EMB)
- After 2 months of treatment, PZA and EMB are discontinued. INH and RIF are continued for another 4 – 7 months or longer.

diagnosis of diphtheria

management of MRSA

diagnosis of mononucleosis

- pharyngeal infection:
  - white or gray glossy exudate in the back of the throat
  - mild sore throat
  - serosanguinous or purulent discharge
- Skin infection is often indistinguishable from other chronic skin diseases.
- cardiac symptoms (myocarditis), neuropathies, or renal failure in severe cases

antibiotics, including trimethoprim (Primsol), sulfamethoxazole (Bactrim), clindamycin (Cleocin), or linezolid (Zyvox)

- fatigue lasting from a few weeks to months
- fever
- pharyngitis
- palatal petechiae
- lymphadenopathy
- airway obstruction
- adenopathy (posterior cervical, auricular, inguinal)
- splenic rupture
- positive mononuclear spot test

diagnosis of pertussis

management of vancomycin-resistant enterococci

diagnosis of tuberculosis

- rapid bouts of coughing followed by hallmark "whoop"
- hoarseness
- increase in mucus
- nausea and vomiting
- choking spells in infants
- positive test for pertussis bacterium

---

antibiotics, including amoxicillin, ampicillin, gentamicin, penicillin, piperacillin, or streptomycin

---

- prolonged productive cough
- general s/s of fever
- night sweats
- hemoptysis
- dyspnea
- positive TB skin test
- multinodular infiltrate on CXR

TWO: PROFESSIONAL ISSUES

medical futility

involuntary commitment

medical interventions that are not likely to result in significant positive outcomes for the patient; interventions that maintain permanent states of unconsciousness

a legal process under which a physician determines that a patient is unsafe to themselves or others and requires close observation under medical care for the sake of safety

evidence-based practice

discharge planning

advance directives

the use of high-quality research outcomes to inform clinical practice; implemented through the establishment of a clinical practice guideline (CPG), either at the local organization or professional association (such as the Emergency Nurses Association) level

In the ED, discharge planning generally consists of arranging for follow-up care either with primary care services or specialty care consultations; patients discharged from the ED are considered stable and should not require extensive discharge planning services.

written statements of individuals' wishes with regard to medical treatment decisions such as resuscitation, intubation, and other interventions; ensure the wishes of the individual are carried out in the event the person is unable to express those wishes at the time of care

do not resuscitate (DNR)

allow natural death (AND)

powers of attorney

No heroic measures should be taken to sustain the patient's life.

The patient does not want any intervention that may sustain life or prevent a natural progression to death.

designates an individual to make decisions in place of the patient when the patient does not have the capacity to do so

family presence policies

sexual assault nurse examiners
(SANE nurses)

common safety issues/errors in ED

Generally, family presence, even during invasive procedures and resuscitation, is recommended; evidence shows that family members assert that it is their preference and right to be present for these efforts, especially in the case of pediatric care.

registered nurses who have completed specialized certification and training for clinical practice in medical forensic care of patients and alleged perpetrators; should be used whenever possible to collect evidence for a rape kit

- patient falls
- medication errors
- ED overcrowding

EMTALA

HIPAA

informed consent

any patient presenting to an ED requesting care must at a minimum receive the following:

- medical screening exam performed by a qualified medical provider (RN does not qualify)
- If the exam reveals a condition requiring immediate or near-immediate care, the patient must be appropriately treated or transferred.

requires that individual health care providers and health care organizations make every attempt to safeguard the protected health information (PHI) of the patient; the minimum amount of PHI needed to accomplish a task should be shared

used in situations where moderately invasive or high-risk procedures are going to be performed; the provider must cover key elements for informed consent to be valid:

- description of the procedure
- risks and benefits of the procedure
- alternative options available to the patient

implied consent

guidelines for pediatric consent

START triage categories

given in situations where patients are at risk to lose life or limb, and they are unable to provide informed consent; only applicable during resuscitation and is no longer implied if the patient is able to give and/or express informed consent

The legal custodian of the pediatric patient must provide consent. Treatment can be provided without custodian consent in some situations:

- immediate danger to life or limb
- STIs or similar issues
- high suspicion of non-accidental trauma or domestic abuse (consent for treatment is implied until the local child services system can determine temporary legal guardianship terms)

- Expectant: Black color. The patient is unlikely to survive injuries despite efforts to resuscitate. Palliative care measures only.
- Immediate: Red color. Patients require immediate intervention with reasonable expectation of preserving life.
- Delayed: Yellow color. Patient's transport and care can be delayed. May include serious, potentially emergent injuries, but deterioration is not imminent.
- Minor: Green color. "The walking wounded." Immediate care is not needed; these patients have relatively minor injuries and can wait for treatment.

THREE: PATHOPHYSIOLOGY

pericardial tamponade

pleural effusion

a buildup of fluid in the pericardial space; the pressure from the fluid prevents the ventricles from functioning properly, compromising cardiac filling and output

the buildup of fluid around the lungs in the pleural space; the fluid buildup can displace lung tissue and inhibit adequate ventilation and lung expansion

preeclampsia

multiple sclerosis (MS)

aortic dissection

syndrome is characterized by hypertension in the mother paired with either proteinuria or end-organ dysfunction

Patches of demyelination (the loss of the protective myelin along neurons) in the brain and the spinal cord cause a delay or a failure of signals in the neurological system and lead to neurological deficits.

a tear in the innermost layer of the aorta that allows blood to enter the aortic media; when the pressure compresses the aortic lumen, blood flow through the vessels is reduced, leading to ischemia of distal tissues and organs

pancreatitis

retinal artery occlusion

neurogenic shock

caused by the release of digestive enzymes into the tissues of the pancreas; causes autodigestion, inflammation, tissue destruction, and injury to adjacent structures and organs

a blockage of vascular flow through the retinal arteries, resulting in a lack of oxygen delivery to the nerve cells in the retina; may occur from thrombi or emboli, and is sometimes referred to as an ocular stroke

a form of shock caused by an injury or trauma to the spinal cord, typically above the level of T6; disrupts the functioning of the automatic nervous system, producing massive vasodilation

pulseless electrical activity (PEA)

esophageal varices

supraventricular tachycardias (SVT)

an organized rhythm without a pulse: the monitor shows an electrical rhythm, but the heart is not functioning

bleeding from veins in the esophagus that dilate and rupture from increased portal pressure caused by liver disease

dysrhythmias with > 100 bpm and a narrow QRS complex (< 0.12 seconds); the dysrhythmia originates at or above the bundle of His (supraventricular); also called narrow complex tachycardia

pyloric stenosis

carotid stenosis

disseminated intravascular
coagulopathy (DIC)

obstruction of gastric outflow that occurs when the pylorus muscle becomes thick and swollen, preventing food from moving to the small intestine

narrowing or hardening of the carotid arteries, usually caused by atherosclerosis

a coagulation disorder with simultaneous intervals of clotting and bleeding

croup

costochondritis

chronic obstructive pulmonary disease
(COPD)

upper airway obstruction caused by subglottic inflammation that results from viral illness; inflammation results in edema in the trachea, and thick, tenacious mucus further obstructs the airway

the inflammation of the costal cartilage, which joins the ribs to the sternum; usually affects the fourth, fifth, and sixth ribs

a breakdown in alveolar tissue (emphysema), chronic productive cough (chronic bronchitis), and long-term obstruction of the airways that worsens over time

hemothorax

muscular dystrophy (MD)

hyperosmolar hyperglycemic state (HHS)

collection of blood in the pleural space

a genetic disorder in which there is a mutation in the recessive dystrophin gene on the X chromosome; causes muscle fiber degeneration, which results in progressive proximal muscle weakness

a severe hyperglycemic state characterized by profound hyperosmolarity and the absence of acidosis; HHS develops gradually over days to weeks; volume depletion occurs as the result of osmotic diuresis caused by prolonged hyperglycemia; more common in persons with type 2 diabetes

Guillain-Barré syndrome

meningitis

placenta previa

a rare autoimmune disorder in which the immune system attacks healthy cells within the nervous system, affecting motor function; can be emergent when respiratory muscles are affected

inflammation of the meninges of the brain and spinal cord

when the placenta partially or completely covers the internal orifice of the cervix

acute adrenal insufficiency
(Addisonian crisis)

autonomic dysreflexia

diffuse axonal injury (DAI)

The adrenal cortex cannot produce enough corticosteroids to meet the body's needs; there is usually an acute escalation of preexisting adrenal insufficiency but this can also be caused by trauma to the adrenal glands.

an overstimulation of the autonomic nervous system, can follow spinal cord injuries above the T6 level; occurs when a sympathetic stimulation to the lower portion of the body leads to vasoconstriction below the area of injury and pushes blood to the upper part of the body

widespread damage to axons in the white matter if the soft tissue of the brain rapidly accelerates or decelerates

intussusception

orchitis

penile fracture

mechanical bowel obstruction caused when a loop of the large intestine telescopes within itself, cutting off the blood supply, causing perforation, infection, and bowel ischemia

inflammation of the testes caused by a bacterial or viral infection; can occur secondary to epididymitis (epididymo-orchitis)

a rupture of the corpus cavernosum and the tunica albuginea, usually as a result of abrupt bending of the erect penis

eclampsia

umbilical cord prolapse

diabetic ketoacidosis (DKA)

onset of tonic-clonic seizures in women with preeclampsia

The cord presents alongside (occult) or ahead of (overt) the presenting fetus during delivery.

hyperglycemic state characterized by an insulin deficiency that stimulates the breakdown of adipose tissues; results in the production of ketones and leads to metabolic acidosis; develops quickly (< 24 hours) and is most common in people with type 1 diabetes

thyrotoxic crisis (thyroid storm)

idiopathic thrombocytopenic purpura (ITP)

myasthenia gravis (MG)

a rapid increase in circulating thyroid hormones; the surge in hormones speeds up metabolism in all body systems and increases oxygen demand

an autoimmune disorder that reduces the life span of platelets; also called immune thrombocytopenia

an autoimmune disorder that causes cell-mediated destruction of acetylcholine receptors that disrupts neuromuscular transmitters, causing episodic muscle weakness and fatigue

acute renal failure (ARF)

labyrinthitis

Ménière's disease

an acute decrease in the kidneys' ability to filter the blood

- prerenal: decreased renal perfusion
- intrinsic renal: disease within the kidneys
- postrenal: blocked drainage of urine

occurs in the inner ear when the vestibulocochlear nerve (eighth cranial nerve) becomes inflamed as the result of either bacterial or viral infection; affects hearing, balance, and spatial navigation

the result of chronic excess fluid in the inner ear; causes the endolymphatic space to enlarge, increasing inner ear pressure and possibly rupturing the inner membrane

trigeminal neuralgia (tic douloureux)

Ludwig's angina

HELLP syndrome

a condition of the trigeminal nerve (fifth cranial nerve) that causes unilateral stabbing, shooting pain and burning sensations along the nerve branches; paroxysms can affect any or all of the three nerve branches: ophthalmic, maxillary, and mandibular

a gangrenous cellulitis that attacks the soft tissue of the neck and the floor of the mouth, generally following an abscess of the second and third molars or other dental infection; the bacterial infection is fast moving and causes extensive edema of the neck and mouth, which can place the patient at high risk for airway obstruction

a form of preeclampsia characterized by hemolysis (H), elevated liver enzymes (EL), and low platelet count (LP)

hyphema

ulcerative keratitis

compartment syndrome

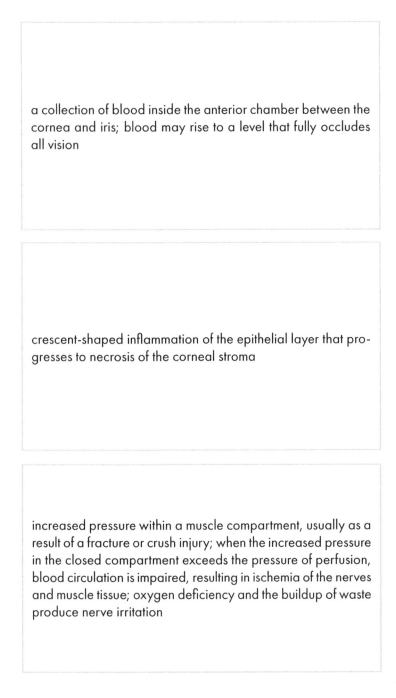

a collection of blood inside the anterior chamber between the cornea and iris; blood may rise to a level that fully occludes all vision

crescent-shaped inflammation of the epithelial layer that progresses to necrosis of the corneal stroma

increased pressure within a muscle compartment, usually as a result of a fracture or crush injury; when the increased pressure in the closed compartment exceeds the pressure of perfusion, blood circulation is impaired, resulting in ischemia of the nerves and muscle tissue; oxygen deficiency and the buildup of waste produce nerve irritation

acute respiratory distress syndrome
(ARDS)

joint effusion

abruptio placentae (placental abruption)

sudden and progressive form of NPE in which the alveoli fill with fluid because of damage to the pulmonary endothelium

The normally small amount of fluid in the synovial compartment of a joint increases; the additional fluid can be the result of infection, inflammation (often from an autoimmune condition), or trauma.

when the placenta separates from the uterus after the twentieth week of gestation but before delivery; can lead to emergent conditions, including hemorrhage and DIC

osteomyelitis

subungual hematoma

immersion foot

an infection in the bone that can occur directly (after a traumatic bone injury) or indirectly (via the vascular system or other infected tissues)

vascular leakage of blood and serous fluid accumulates under the nail bed of the upper or lower phalanges

the result of prolonged exposure to a cold and wet environment of a limb that had little or no mobility; the cold causes vasoconstriction of the blood vessels, leading to spasms and ischemia of the vascular system and damage to the vascular and nerve tissue in the affected limb

testicular torsion

Bell's palsy

chilblains

occurs when the spermatic cord, which supplies blood to the testicles, becomes twisted, leading to an ischemic testicle

a unilateral facial paralysis or weakness caused by inflammation of the facial nerve (seventh cranial nerve)

an inflammatory response that occurs in the skin and small blood vessels as a result of repeated exposure to cold but not freezing temperatures; most commonly seen in women, underweight patients, and patients with Raynaud's disease

diabetes insipidus

acute angle-closure glaucoma

Clostridium difficile (C. diff.)

a deficiency of antidiuretic hormone (ADH) (also called vaso-pressin) produced by the posterior lobe of the pituitary gland; ADH deficiency affects the renal tubules' ability to concentrate urine, causing large amounts of undiluted urine to be excreted from the body

intraocular pressure increases rapidly to 30 mm Hg or higher (normal pressure is 8 – 21 mm Hg); permanent vision loss from compression of the optic nerve can occur in as little as a few hours if not rapidly treated

an acute bacterial infection in the intestine most commonly seen after antibiotic use, which disrupts the normal intestinal flora, allowing the antibiotic-resistant C. diff spores to proliferate in the intestines; the bacterium releases a toxin that causes the intestine to produce yellow-white plaques on the intestinal lining

FOUR: QUICK RESPONSE

What medication is administered for treatment of acetaminophen overdose?

What is the first-line pharmaceutical treatment for status epilepticus?

N-acetylcysteine

benzodiazepines (e.g., diazepam, lorazepam, or midazolam)

Bowel sounds heard in the lung fields are associated with what condition?

Severe headache, often described as the worst pain the patient has ever experienced, is associated with what condition?

The CEN may delegate tasks to which personnel in the ED?

diaphragm rupture

subarachnoid hemorrhage

LPNs/LVNs, paramedics and EMTs working in the ED, medical assistants, nursing assistants, and technicians

What medication will likely be administered to a hemodynamically stable patient diagnosed with a pulmonary embolus?

Battle's sign, hemotympanum, and raccoon eyes are associated with what condition?

What serious complications should be monitored in a patient with pancreatitis?

heparin

basilar skull fracture

respiratory complications, including ARDS and atelectasis

Kussmaul respirations and ketones in urine are associated with what condition?

Tracheal deviation, distended neck veins, and decreased breath sounds are associated with what condition?

What medication is given to decrease portal hypertension in patients with esophageal varices?

diabetic ketoacidosis

tension pneumothorax

octreotide (Sandostatin)

Sudden, unilateral, painless loss of vision in one eye is associated with what condition?

What medication should the nurse expect to administer to a patient with diabetes insipidus?

What medications will likely be administered to a patient with ischemic chest pain and no changes to the ST segment or T wave?

retinal artery occlusion

vasopressin (ADH)

aspirin and nitroglycerin; morphine may be given for additional pain relief

Defibrillation is indicated for which cardiac rhythms?

Discharge for a patient with diverticulitis should include education on what type of diet?

What is the priority intervention for neurogenic shock?

ventricular tachycardia (V-tach) and ventricular fibrillation (V-fib)

a liquid diet followed by a low-fiber diet until the inflammation is reduced, then a high-fiber diet to prevent straining

IV fluid resuscitation

In what circumstances should chain of custody procedures be followed?

What is the definitive treatment for an infant with pyloric stenosis?

What lab results are associated with DIC?

when a crime is known or suspected to have been committed, including GSWs; trauma; sexual assault; and domestic, child, or elder abuse

surgery

thrombocytopenia, prolonged clotting times (PT and PTT), decreased fibrinogen, and increased levels of fibrinolysis products (D-dimer and FSP)

What is the first-line intervention for ischemic priapism?

Why is magnesium administered to pregnant patients with hypertension and proteinuria?

In the START triage system, which patients are coded with the color red?

aspiration with intracavernosal phenylephrine injection

to prevent seizure (eclampsia)

patients requiring immediate intervention with reasonable
expectation of preserving life

Sudden, severe, and tearing pain in the chest that radiates to the back is associated with what condition?

When can a nurse assume implied consent for a patient?

What interventions should the nurse anticipate for a patient with unstable SVT?

aortic dissection

situations where patients risk losing life or limb, and they are unable to provide informed consent

synchronized cardioversion

Under what circumstances can a patient's surrogate or medical power of attorney make medical decisions for the patient?

In adults, an S3 sound is associated with dysfunction in which area of the heart?

What lung sounds are associated with pneumonia?

when the patient does not have the capacity to make medical decisions

ventricular dysfunction (e.g., heart failure, dilated cardiomy-opathy)

decreased lung sounds and inspiratory crackles in affected lung

What sound can be heard during auscultation of a patient with pericarditis?

What diagnostic test should the nurse anticipate for a patient with s/s of a stroke?

What medication should the nurse expect to administer to a patient experiencing an exacerbation of COPD?

friction rub

CT scan to rule out hemorrhage

bronchodilator (e.g., albuterol)

Hemoptysis is most commonly associated with what condition?

A patient diagnosed with hemorrhagic stroke has a secure airway and is currently hemodynamically stable. What is the nursing priority when caring for this patient?

A patient presents with dull, steady periumbilical pain in the RLQ, positive Rovsing's sign, positive psoas sign, and fever. What intervention should the nurse anticipate?

pulmonary edema

monitoring for and treating ICP

surgery for appendicitis

Made in the USA
Coppell, TX
18 September 2022